Confessions of an intercessor

My first 35 years with the God of miracles

Kent Boström

Publishing house: BoD – Books on Demand, Stockholm, Sweden

Print: BoD – Books on Demand, Norderstedt, Gemany

ISBN: 978-91-7969-190-5

This book is also available in Swedish:
En förebedjares bekännelser (ISBN: 9789180076784)

Foreword

Have you ever considered how complex a human being is? After spending just a few minutes with someone, our picture of that person is quite clear. Still, we have no idea what that person carries, regarding memories, impressions, and experiences.

The reason for mentioning this is because it relates to what is about to unfold in this book. I will be sharing with you some occurrences that have shaken my world completely and affected my whole life. There are miracles described in detail and some of them include life-threatening situations.

After much contemplation, I have decided to publish these stories in a book, and now it is accomplished. Some things may not be very particular to you, while other stories could have had a different ending, had they happened to you.

I understand that my 'baggage' and my values might differ a bit from yours. This becomes clear when you try to share your own experiences, some of which are on the inside and may not be visible to the people around you. One powerful experience for me might be quite 'flat' for others to read about. Despite that risk, I have stepped out of my comfort zone and have given this a try.

What is an intercessor?

The word "intercessor" is not used very often, particularly not outside the church context. I like the Swedish term *"förebedjare"* better. It translates to *"foreprayer"* and describes a person who is praying for people and circumstances, causing a positive change.

With this, I welcome you to get a glimpse of my world. Here we go…

Index

Appendix

1. Introduction

Briefly about Kent

I am born and raised in a city called Eskilstuna, Sweden, in quite an ordinary working-class family. We were certainly not rich, but there was always food on the table and we had roof over our heads. The only time I encountered Christian faith as a child was when I met my grandfather Rudolf, who was an old Pentecostal man.

Rudolf was a man of prayer, but this I knew nothing about as a little boy. Back then, every meal in his house was started by a grace song, which amazed me every time. So, my experience of Christianity was not big.

At a young age, I often kept to myself and did not have many friends. The advantage was that I became quite independent of what others thought of me and did not have to consider peer pressure so often. I discovered the social part later and nowadays I love getting to know new people.

My journey through life has not followed a straight line, rather has it been a difficult journey. It has been filled with both ups and downs, foolish decisions, and successful strategies.

I have also experienced a large portion of Grace from God, that is, to receive something without deserving it. I think you will agree with this after reading.

2. Electric oil?

*There and then, something happened
that changed my life completely*

Back in 1980, I decided to become a Christian and joined a local church in Eskilstuna. A few years down the road, I concluded that it was not really my style. It was too rigid and 'religious' for my liking. I respect those who enjoy that kind of environment, but it was not for me.

Two years had passed, with numerous church services attended. Mostly, they comprised of singing ancient hymns and listening to preaching that did not move me. I was not impressed. Eventually, I began to question whether this was all there is to the Christian life. Where were the miracles that the Bible talks about? And why did my prayers feel like a one-way communication?

One day, back home from church, I sat down on the couch and prayed, opened my heart, and said: *"I'm sorry Lord, but if this is all You have to offer, I'm not interested. If You have something more, please show it to me, or I will skip this. Just attending boring church services and living this kind of life is not for me. I have another life to live".*

It was a simple, but brutally honest, prayer. No preconceived notions and no demands, I just wanted to know if what I had seen so far was everything. So, I skipped the 'church life' and ceased attending services.

A few years later, during spring 1985, I got to know some other Christian people. They seemed to have a completely different experience of Christian life than mine. When they read from the Bible, the text was somehow more alive to them than to me.

One day, they asked if I wanted to join them in attending a Christian conference meeting, listening to a famous preacher on Saturday. Having nothing planned for the weekend, I reluctantly agreed. I even remember the exact date; it was 21st April 1985.

The conference took place in an ice hockey arena, rented for the occasion. When we arrived, we were not allowed to enter. I found this very strange. Later, I was told that a girl in our party had behaved badly and disturbed previous meetings so much that she had been barred from the conference. Despite her protests, she was not admitted. Out of respect for her, the ushers did not explain this to the rest of us. The situation became so awkward that I decided to skip the meeting. What kind of strange people were these?

It was a disappointment, driving for an hour then not being admitted, but it was a fact. Going back to the car, we noticed that Hannu, who came with us, had entered the meeting without us. I went to find him but was stopped by an usher. Worship had started so I was not allowed to enter. The meeting would last for about two hours. Meanwhile, we took refuge at McDonalds, waiting for the time to pass. What an anti-climax!

Two hours later, we drove back to pick up Hannu, only to find the meeting had not finished yet. The place was full of people and I managed to sneak in. There was an empty place in one of the back corners. The PA system was quite insufficient, not much was heard from the stage. With a crowd obscuring the view, I didn't see too much neither. When it was time to pray, I did what I always did during prayer; clasped my hands, closed my eyes, and thought about God.

There and then, something happened that changed my life completely.

There is no description for what hit me – words fail me. The closest I can get is to say it was like electrical oil being poured over my head. Whatever it was, it filled me completely in a way that cannot be described.

I opened my eyes, trying to see what had caused this. A friend of mine sat next to me and saw something happening to me. He asked what it was. *"I have no idea. Here, feel this!"*

I took his hand; it was as if he was electrocuted and startled.

I knew (and I think you understand also), an electric shock could not be the cause since neither a power cable, nor a connector, were nearby. And no oil either, for that matter. When I went back to the car afterwards, I was very puzzled over this.

As I sat down behind the steering wheel, the next strange thing happened. Hannu, who had been in the meeting, now sat in the front seat next to me and was somehow filled by God's presence. He was shining like a powerful lamp; I was almost dazzled by the light! Had he walked in front of the car, in the dark, I would have seen the road in that light. I will never forget that day.

The coming months included several experiences with the presence of God, so powerful that even now, I fail to describe them. It was like He said: *"You wanted more? How about this?"* He heard my simple prayer years ago and had been waiting for the right moment.

After this, I started to read the Bible with a new attitude. What if it held a truth that I had failed to see earlier? How much of it can I implement into my own life? How close can you be to Jesus in your everyday life?

I decided to find out.

My journey with the God of miracles had begun.

3. Medical problems

"Had you arrived an hour later,the boy would have been dead by now!"

In the early 60's, before my first birthday, I became seriously ill. I couldn't tolerate the gruel and it got worse and worse. It led to an acute ileus because my small intestine got twisted around itself. Mum was worried that I was screaming incessantly and seemed to be in bad shape, so she called a doctor and asked for advice.

"No worries, it's just colic," said the first doctor.

After a while, my face started to turn blue, so my mother decided to call another doctor.

"That sounds serious, I'm sending for an ambulance at once," was the answer from the second doctor. The ambulance soon arrived and took us to the hospital.

There was surgery immediately and they managed to straighten the ileus. I was in such poor condition that they could not put an intravenous therapy drip into my arm but had to make an incision in the skin of my leg to find a blood vessel. The scar is still there today, a few centimetres long, below my right knee.

Afterwards, the doctor stated that I would not have survived another hour without medical care. The name of the second doctor was Birger Wictorin, I have him to thank for my life.

Was my rescue supernatural? My answer is both yes and no. Mum realised that something was seriously wrong and did what any parent would've done. But it's also true that my grandfather Rudolf was a man of prayer who prayed for all his children and grandchildren every day. My belief is that his prayers helped us to arrive at the hospital in time.

After this came a period with many visits to the hospital; I even celebrated my first birthday there. I don't remember anything myself, but I still have the small teddy bear that a nurse gave me for a birthday present. You see, back then, parents were not allowed to stay as they are, and often do, today. They were only admitted during visiting hours. It must have been a gloomy time for both Mum and Dad.

As I grew up, I had continuous health problems. Among other issues, I didn't grow quite as I should. I was often lacking power and had several diffuse symptoms. Sometimes I was hospitalised just for samples to be taken. Blood samples, urine samples, all kind of samples were taken. On a few occasions I was there for up to a week without the medical staff being able to find any major fault.

One special memory was when a newly hired nurse told me that she would pinch me in the arm a little. *"You mean, you need blood for the ESR, right?"* I said calmly and put my arm out for the blood to be taken. It was probably not the most common comment she received from a boy who had not even started school.

During my teens, the doctors suspected I had celiac disease, i.e., gluten intolerance. At that time (mid-70's), there was much less knowledge about gluten available than we have at our fingertips today. We can easily find detailed information about what gluten is, what the health effects are, and how to deal with them.

Back then, the information was scarce. Among other things, it was estimated that there were only 30 people with gluten intolerance per 1 million people in Sweden. Today we know that it's quite a common disease. The few gluten free products available in the 70's were both expensive and difficult to find, so cooking became a challenge for my mother.

When I moved away from home, I chose to drop the gluten free diet as it made no major difference to me. In recent years, however, I have chosen to reduce gluten significantly as it makes my stomach calmer. Another reason is, of course, today's large choice of gluten free products and meals in shops and restaurants. My conclusion is that you can be sensitive to gluten without being intolerant.

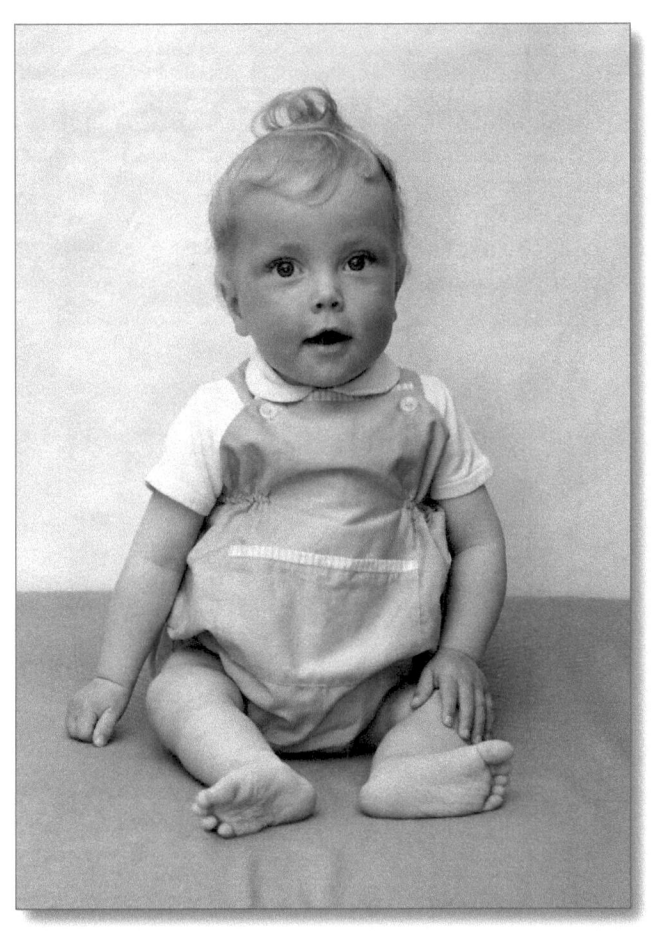

This is me, almost one year old

4. One unnatural fear

...the second after, I experienced a dark shadow leaving me

In 1982 I left home; my first apartment was within walking distance and I paid visits to my mother's house quite often. Walking home one Saturday night, three guys of my age came up to me. They were drunk and looking for a fight. One of them started fighting but he was too drunk to do any harm. Realising that I would never be able to handle them alone, I chose to run instead of fight. They were too drunk to catch up with me, so nothing more happened. At least, that's what I thought…

After that unpleasant experience, it was like a fear, almost panic, clung to me. I couldn't grasp it or shake it off, and it remained with me for several years. When it was at its worst, I could barely walk alone downtown Eskilstuna on a Saturday afternoon. It was a feeling that cannot be described in words. I was considering seeking help from a psychologist, but it never happened and my choice not to tell anyone about it left me alone with the problem.

By this time, I had started to hang out with a group of Christian people, who had a living faith in Jesus. There was something in their way of expecting answers to their prayers that made me very curious. One Saturday evening in May 1985, we were gathered for a prayer meeting. A guy named Ronald asked if he could pray for me, and I was happy to accept it. Ronald put a hand on my head and began praying.

Suddenly, without a warning, he commanded the fear to let me go. I didn't have time to react to what he did or said, but the very second after, I experienced a dark shadow leaving me. It was so real that I still remember that feeling today. It was like having a black cloth over your head, and then taking it off in one swift move.

Afterwards, Ronald told me about the prophetic appeal from God he had received, to pray for me and the unnatural fear I was carrying. He did not know about any of my fears since I had not told anyone about it.

Was it really gone now? It would soon become obvious as it was time to catch the late bus and go home. Knowing that the bus would remain for a longer stop in the middle of central Eskilstuna on a Saturday night had tormented me earlier, but still I chose to go to the prayer meeting. As I was sitting on the bus, all my senses switched to full alert, searching for possible threats that could arise.

After just a few seconds, I relaxed. That unnatural fear really had disappeared from my life! I remained sitting on the bus, completely calm - even when the driver got off for a smoke and left the doors open. That feeling of panic never came back.

Afterwards, I have experienced several situations that have been both unpleasant and dangerous, but that strong fear, the panic, has never managed to get hold of me again. Had I seen a psychologist, I would probably have been diagnosed with post-traumatic stress disorder, PTSD. But a diagnosis of that kind would only explain the physical and psychological nature of my problem.

The cause of my problem was spiritual and disappeared after prophetic intercession. Today, 35 years later, I have no problems at all with that panicky fear I felt for three years.

I am free!

5. The New Life

A new world is opening up

In the spring of 1985, I began to seek God's presence more actively. After experiencing it so powerfully, I wanted to know what more there was to receive from Heaven. With an endless appetite for the New Life, I attended numerous prayer meetings, services, and Christian conferences. After enjoying one teaching, I often bought the cassette tape recording from that meeting. Also, I subscribed to several cassette series with bible teachings.

At that time, I worked on a factory floor in Eskilstuna (at a subsidiary of Bahco Tools, producing pliers). With a sedentary and monotonous factory job came the opportunity to listen to cassette tapes during work. Each morning I listened to Christian worship music until breakfast, and then the Bible study started.

One of the favourite topics is the righteousness we have through Jesus. When Jesus died for us on the cross, the door to God was opened. This means that we can have fellowship with Him in a way that must be experienced as it cannot be explained. The Bible says, in John 1:12, *"Yet to all who did receive him, to those who believed in his name, he gave the right to become children of God."*

After lunch I had the time for another teaching session before my workday was over. It was like having my own little Bible school at work and I enjoyed every minute of it. The presence of God came almost immediately when the worship music sounded in my headphones. Several times it was so sweet that it felt like I was halfway to Heaven.

And, it affected my work, in a positive way. Somehow, I managed to do the job faster than anyone else had done before. With a job on the chords, I was soon one of the best paid on the factory floor. The work I did was always perfect. The quality inspector often came and inspected it but never found anything that failed to meet the quality standard.

With the New Life came new discoveries. I discovered more and more that God does not hate me; quite the contrary. He loves me (and everyone on this planet) so much more than we can ever comprehend. That is why Jesus chose to die on the cross, 2000 years ago. He paid the ultimate price for me to have a living relationship with the Father.

My next discovery was that He wants to be a part of my life and not just a spectator. One of many examples was when I finally managed to quit smoking cigarettes. I had tried many times before without success, but this time I managed to win the battle. The nicotine craving was a tough competitor, but finally came the day when I quit for good. I even remember the date, it was a Friday, 17th May 1986. It took over three months before the urge to smoke disappeared completely, but it sure was worth the fight.

As the years passed, I began to understand that God is good. I mean, *really good*. In His wonderful presence, I hear and understand His guidance more clearly. My favourite way to stay close to Jesus is to listen to worship music. Everywhere I go, I keep music from Hillsong, Phil Driscoll, and alike, with me. As strange as it may sound, I am walking in His presence, and enjoying every second of it!

6. Moving to Haninge

Time for a new place

During spring of 1987, I came to a turning point in my life. It was time for me to take a new step in my walk with Jesus. Maybe study at a Bible school? Many of my Christian friends attended, or had attended, Bible school. I had multiple choices to consider.

One day I heard about a small local church in the city of Haninge, south of Stockholm, and became curious to know more about it. I phoned the church and spoke to one of their volunteers and was welcomed to visit. On the day in April, when I planned to visit them, they were going to have a Bible study. I was given travel directions and a few days later it was time to go there.

A good friend joined me for the 90 minutes car drive. When we arrived, the teaching had taken a short break, so our timing was perfect. The pastor, Stefan Swärd, came up to us and introduced himself. He encouraged me to move to the area and asked the attendants if anyone could help me find a place to live.

We were invited to participate in the following lesson and were happy to accept. I had a clear feeling that this was the right place for me. After spending less than one hour here, I decided to move to this area. It was an easy decision to make.

Immediately after the meeting, one guy came up to me and told me about a room he rented from an elderly lady in the church. He was planning to move out in a few months and then his room would be vacant. He took me to the house so I could have a look at it. Despite being just a room, it was exactly what I needed.

Finding accommodation, the one thing I had worried about the most, was resolved at once. I moved in on the 1st of August 1987. I have lived in this city since then, except for the years 1996-98, when my studies took me back to Eskilstuna.

Finding a new job was quickly arranged. At that time, there were so many jobs available that the Swedish Public Employment Service even went out to the residential areas with mobile offices, encouraging people applying for jobs.

I learned that the southern suburbs of Stockholm holds the lowest percentage of people attending a Christian church on regular basis, in the whole country of Sweden. It really was a pioneer work ongoing in the area.

At church I found my spiritual home, something I had missed in Eskilstuna. Most of the church members where new to this area, just like me. In the years that followed, the church membership grew and was active with, among other things, tent meetings next to a mini golf course.

It was exciting to invite people to the tent and see how the visitors were touched by God's presence at the meetings. On the days of the tent meetings, there were unusually many who wanted to play mini golf on the adjacent course in the evenings. We had a good PA system so everyone within 200 meters distance from the tent heard both the worship music and the preaching clearly.

I remember one evening, I left the tent in the middle of the meeting to collect something from my car. The mini golf course was full of people playing, but none of the players spoke to each other as everyone wanted to hear the ongoing preaching.

I believe man is created for fellowship with God and that there is a longing in the heart of men that cannot be satisfied by anything else. That longing became obvious to me during this time.

The tent in Brandbergen 1990. It will be a few hours before
the meeting starts. The signs say, "JESUS GIVES JOY".

7. Forgiveness

The feeling of freedom

A large part of Christian teaching is about forgiveness. A search for the word *"forgive"* and its variants yields over 120 hits in the Bible. Jesus speaks of forgiveness numerous times; the most dramatic moment is found in Luke 23:34. It describes how Jesus hangs on the cross and is mocked by those who got him convicted after presenting false accusations. Yet, He says, *"Father, forgive them, for they do not know what they are doing."*

His statement feels totally incomprehensible to the human way of reasoning, but we get an understanding of how much Jesus loves all human beings.

When I grew up, I hosted a reluctance to forgive people who had hurt me in some way, especially if they did not ask for my forgiving. I tightly held onto my right to be angry about what had happened.

After being Christian for some time, I began to accept the teaching of forgiving. Forgiveness does not mean that I give my approval for what has happened. However, it helps me to let go of the bad memory, so it no longer bothers me. Forgiving is not a feeling but a decision. First, I must start by wanting to forgive an injustice, no matter what my feelings are. Once that decision is made, it is easier to letting go of it emotionally as well.

Here I am talking about forgiveness in general. I have not experienced any particularly horrible things in my life. For a while, I thought a lot about what things I needed to forgive people for. Later, I realised that my entire life story does not need to undergo an investigation.

Today, if a troublesome memory pops up, I address it at once. After concluding that a person did something wrong, I choose to forgive that very person. The whole thing is settled in less than a minute, the person concerned does not even need to know about it. If the memory comes back again, I remind myself that this particular person is already forgiven. It's a simple but effective process and has helped me to let go of difficult memories.

This brings another memory to my mind, of a woman, C, who left me just a few months before we were supposed to be getting married. It happened in 1989 and, quite obviously, broke my heart. The whole story is so tedious, so I am going to skip the details. Shortly afterwards, she moved to another city, so I didn't see her very often. Almost 30 years passed before we met again.

My wife Britta and I had started socialising with the same people as C and her husband. It was like my inner man jolted every time we met, it became like a knot in my stomach. Both my wife Britta and C's husband knew the story and what had happened between us. But one day, the opportunity arose to speak about what happened so many years ago. I got the chance to share my view of the experience and how it had affected me.

When C gave her perspective, I got a deeper understanding of what I had anticipated all these years. We simply did not fit together. She sincerely asked me to forgive her. I had already forgiven her 100 times and now I had the opportunity to do it in person, face-to-face.

This was a turning point for me. My active choice to forgive her allowed me to let go of everything, once and for all. Some weeks later, I ran into C in a shopping mall. We chatted for a few minutes before moving on, walking in opposite directions. When we parted, I realised the knot in my stomach that had plagued me previously, was gone. I was free!

The principles of forgiving worked once again, despite taking so many years before the story came to a proper end. If there is one thing I really appreciate about the New Life, it is the teaching of forgiveness. It has changed my life!

8. The London Adventure

I have never run so fast in my life!

In the late summer of 1988, our church received visitors from a local church from a London suburb. They were attending a Bible school called *TIE*, Training In Evangelism. Staying for two weeks, we did a lot of evangelistic outreach together with them and shared many fun moments.

During the following months, I kept in touch with some of them and got invited to visit them in Cobham, located some 23 miles (37 km) southwest of London. I received an invitation to celebrate the New Year with them and gladly accepted. I looked forward to the first flight of my life. The journey went well, and they picked me up at Gatwick Airport on the afternoon of New Year's Eve. It was a nice celebration in a mansion with over 100 happy people.

When my friends were at work during the week, I had plenty of time to explore London on my own. One evening, I went to see a musical with another person from their church. We saw Starlight Express, a very fast-paced show. Tracks had been built around the entire theatre where the actors, playing the various locomotives, rode around on roller skates. The evening came to an end and it was time for me to go back.

Earlier, I had consulted the timetable and knew that the last commuter train back to Cobham would leave Waterloo Station shortly after midnight, at 00:10. Arriving at Waterloo around 23:30, I went to check the timetable again. Maybe I could catch an earlier train?

Imagine my surprise when I looked at the timetable and realized that I was totally wrong – the last train had already left and would **arrive in Cobham** at 00:10!

Almost every ticket booth was closed but there was one open, so I asked for advice. Maybe I could take a night bus instead? *"There are no buses at night, the next bus leaves at 05:00. But the last train is leaving for Effingham Junction in two minutes,"* the ticket seller replied. Wow, Effingham Junction, where was that? There was no time to investigate…

Would it even be possible to make it to the train in time, in the other end of this large station? I have never run so fast in my life! When I arrived, the doors of the train closed. The conductor was about to step into his booth in the last carriage. *"Are you coming?"* he asked, opening his door so I could enter. Out of breath, I stepped onboard without being able to ask where we were going.

"I'm going to Cobham, is it close?" I asked when I was able to talk again. The conductor chuckled. *"No, it's two miles from Effingham Junction,"* he replied. *"Well, that's not too far, it's walking distance,"* I muttered to myself and received a strange look from him.

"No worries, I'm from Sweden and we are used to walking," I tried to explain. He gave me a puzzled look and let me into the passenger part of the train. Sitting in the almost empty carriage, I wondered what footpaths I could find. With a bit of luck, it wasn't just highways to Cobham.

As the train arrived at Effingham Junction, the conductor came and offered me a ride home, he had his car parked at the station. Of course, I was very happy to accept his offer. I was incredibly lucky, getting a ride with a friendly person who was not even going to Cobham - he lived in the opposite direction. I didn't have to manage a long walk at night, in an unknown area, after all.

(I later checked the distance between Cobham and Effingham Junction; it turns out to be 3.4 miles, just over 5 km. To walk that distance would take an hour if you knew the way. Back then, we didn't have smart phones with map function, so that walk would have been both a long and difficult one.)

The conductor gave me a lift all the way up to the front door. He was very friendly and rejected any offer of payment for the ride. I had my own key, so I didn't have to wake up my friends when I got home. The next morning, I told them about my nocturnal adventure and the luck of getting a ride all the way back.

They looked at me wide-eyed, then at each other, and then back at me again. *"Luck?! No, you were not lucky, that's a miracle! Everyone knows how grumpy the employees in London's commuter trains can be. Someone offering to drive a person home voluntarily simply doesn't happen!"* they said.

The grace of God had been with me more than I first understood.

A few days later, back in Haninge, I met one of the older ladies from church. Before I even had the chance to say anything, she gave me a sharp eye.

"What have you been up to?!" she asked. *"Several of us have been in prayer for you; we have been very worried. Especially the other day when God urged us to pray extra for you. We gathered some friends just to pray for you. Now you must tell me, what happened?"*

At first, I was a little puzzled over this question as they weren't the anxious kind of people. I told her how I missed the last train to Cobham from Waterloo Station, and how everything worked out so well despite this. When I told her about how I received a lift home, in the middle of the night, with a friendly conductor, she smiled.

"Now I see why we experienced such a strong urge to pray for you for protection. What if you had missed the train, or had to walk the whole long way? But our God is good, he took good care of you!" she said.

I totally agree. God's grace was with me, even in the dark night, south of London. Because some older friends had followed the Bible's word *"Carry each other's burdens"* (Galatians 6: 2), God was able to intervene in my life, once again.

Meeting Benny Hill at the Madame Tussauds wax cabinet in London

9. Wrecked finances

The action paralysis was total…

Would you believe me if I told you, I have been so poor that I had no food to eat for several days? In the autumn of 1992, it happened to me. It all came to a point where I was lying on my bed, just waiting to starve to death. I mean, physically, for real!

I lost my job and had no unemployment insurance or any other income for several months. Finally, the day came when all my resources were gone. The fridge, freezer and pantry were empty, and I was suffering a total paralysis of action. My last penny had gone to pay the electricity bill. At that time, I was single and realized that I was running out of options. There was no hope left.

The financial situation in Sweden was troublesome, with a serious price drop for houses. As a result, my condominium apartment had lost over half of its value and could not be sold. The panic hit, making me isolate more and more from my friends. I couldn't even think clearly enough to seek help from the Social Services Office. My telephone was cut off, so I couldn't call anyone either. Quite simply, I was doomed. In my mind, I began seeing the image of not surviving this challenge…

But God had mercy on me! When all my hope was gone, there was a knock at the door and Eva H, a lady from church, stood outside with a grocery bag. She had a whim to visit me and arrange lunch, without knowing how bad my situation was. I will always be grateful that she followed the voice of her heart, otherwise I have no idea how this story would have ended.

Eva also managed to persuade me to start looking for a job, and a few days later I got a few hours work as a supply teacher in a school. As I got more and more substitute hours, hope began to grow within me – maybe I would be able to fend for myself after all? I also managed to find help at the Social Services Office when my salary was insufficient.

I came to a foreclosure and my apartment was sold at an auction, leaving me with large debts. At this time, the loan interest rate was over 15% per year, so my debts continued to grow.

The road back has been long and filled with wonders, miracles, and failures. I do realise that this misery was caused by my own previous decisions; I bought an apartment without having sufficient finances, and it was my decision to leave the union and its unemployment insurance a few years earlier. Looking back now, it is easy to say these were two incredibly stupid decisions.

The turning point came when I was in Kenya during the autumn of 1995. The whole journey there was a miracle as I could not afford anything – not the travel cost nor the living expenses. When I was in Mombasa, I decided to deal with my personal situation. It was time to get an education so I could get a sensible job and start paying off my debts.

Looking back at the circumstances of my restoration, I see a series of God's wonders and miracles. They came as small, but important, steps in the development. I applied to study computer engineering in Eskilstuna and moved there before the admission was approved. I was still living on social benefits. After sleeping on my friend's sofa for six months, I managed to get a first-hand lease for an apartment. This was possible thanks to my friend Per-Owe, who put some good words in for me with the landlord.

With a new motivation, I took my studies seriously. The result came two years later, when I gained the highest grade in 70% of the subjects. After graduating in 1998, I moved back to Haninge, where my search for employment began. I was expecting to find a job right away, but it was not time for that miracle to take place yet – I realised that later.

It was frustrating not to get an employment offer from any of the 20-30 jobs I'd applied for in the first two months. Finally, I got an assignment as a computer teacher for adults in evening classes. That job paid so well that when I married my Britta, after only six months of saving, we didn't need to borrow one single penny.

About the same time, I got a job at a company called Grindex. I worked there for ten years and now things started to fall into place. God was not content to *'just'* provide a job for me. He has blessed me with a development at work that has been completely impossible without His intervention. I don't think it would been possible with any of the other jobs I'd applied for.

It took many long years of rubbing and struggling with monthly instalments before I was debt free, but in 2013, that day finally came. Twenty years of cleaning up my mess was finally done. Today, my life is lightyears from when I lay hungry on my bed, in the autumn of 1992.

You might be thinking all happy circumstances happened because I was just lucky. Was it really God who helped me? Early in my walk with Jesus, I realised that I need to keep praying until I see things change. The phrase *"pray through"* comes from the Pentecostal revival, almost 100 years ago. They prayed until impossible things happened. (I am writing about how prayer works in the chapter *"Briefly about prayer"*)

There really have been numerous things to *pray through* over the years. As mentioned, I slept on a friend's sofa for several months before my accommodation got settled. Living on social benefits when I was studying was, to say the least, scarce. It is frustrating when you get rejection after rejection, having applied for so many jobs. But on the inside, I knew that a job was on the way, so I never gave up the hope.

I remember one job vacancy particularly well; we were a total of 96 applicants, and I was one of the three final people they would choose from in the end. It was a real disappointment, not being the one who got that job offer. Today, as I look back, I am incredibly grateful for not getting it. If that job had become mine, I would not have seen the development that has characterised my professional life over the past twenty years.

Another turning point was when the Marketing Manager at Grindex offered me a job in a profession for which I did not even have the competence. Leaving my career as an IT technician to learn the principles of marketing by working 'on the job' was incredibly evolving. I took several courses and discovered the profession, piece by piece.

My profession usually requires university qualifications before an employer will consider an applicant, but I only have high school qualifications. When I got the job, I did not even know the job title. For others, my job title is spelled Marketing Communicator; for me, it spells *MIRACLE*!

Grindex submersible dewatering pumps keep water away in one of the locks at Lilla Edet, Southern Sweden, 2009. This picture was published in several trade magazines.

10. *"You are not feeling well, are you?"*

*By the way he looked at me, he
thought I might die any moment.*

In February 1994, I visited Hamburg in Germany for a weekend. On the bus trip back home, I suffered from mild food poisoning after eating something that wasn't properly cooked. It was the catalyst for something else, and much worse. Somehow, my immune system reacted to the insulin producing cells as though they were intruders and began to attack them.

Two months later, symptoms appeared; I was constantly thirsty and needed to pee very often. No matter how much water I drank, the thirst was not quenched. I had to visit the bathroom at least once every hour, feeling my bladder was about to burst. Gradually it grew even worse, with up to eight bathroom visits every night.

Another symptom was my weight loss – over 18 pounds (8 kilos) in two months. It happened gradually so I didn't notice it myself. However, my family and friends did notice it and nagged me to see a doctor. I didn't want to think about it as I wasn't in pain. Eventually, I realised that something wasn't right.

The next symptom was a strange stiffness in my body, and this worried me. Initially, it happened when I was having a rest after lunch and it was time for me to go to the bathroom. My fingers, hands, arms, and legs felt paralyzed. It was the same kind of feeling you get when you get 'pins and needles' in your foot.

Getting out of bed was a challenge and now I had major problems with my fingers. I could barely move them and would hardly have managed something as simple as picking up a pen from the table.

Every visit to the bathroom became increasingly difficult with a bladder that was ready to burst, while hands and fingers hardly working at all. The stiffness appeared when I lay or sat down for a while. Like the other symptoms, it only got worse as time went by.

The constant tiredness forced me to sleep most of the day. For once, I was happy to be unemployed as I would not be able to do any work. Eventually, I arranged for an appointment to see a doctor.

It was the 25th of May, and the sun was shining. Being so weak, I wasn't sure I could manage the 10-minute walk to the doctor's office on my own. A friend came along as moral support. Once I arrived at the doctor's office, they took several blood samples for examination.

Finally, the doctor had an answer. She explained that I suffered from diabetes, type 1. A simple blood sugar test showed that my blood sugar level, before eating anything, was as high as 20 mmol per one litre of blood. The normal is 5-8, and over 15, there is no doubt about diabetes. A non-diabetic person never goes over 15, even after eating grapes or other food with lots of carbohydrates.

I went home to pack my bag and eat. When I arrived at the emergency room at Nacka Hospital, they took good care of me immediately. Intravenous therapy began, and I was transferred to the intensive care unit. Even more samples were taken; blood, urine and my weight were recorded. My blood glucose level was now 25, and I got my first insulin dose. During the next two days at the intensive care unit, I was given over five litres of drip. The doctor later told me that in my dehydrated state, I would not have survived much longer. Several of my blood vessels ruptured during the work of inserting the intravenous therapy.

My body responded immediately having received insulin. The stiffness disappeared soon, and my weight started to increase again. During the first week alone, I gained almost 2 kilos (4 pounds) of weight.

My thirst, and the need to go to the bathroom, quickly returned to normal levels. I could feel the strength in my body resuming. After a few days, I had recovered a lot and was able to take short walks outside the hospital. I remained in the hospital for a week to ensure the insulin doses were set properly.

Another discovery at the hospital was that I had Addison's disease. It is a rare long-term endocrine disorder and one of the symptoms is an unnatural tiredness, just like the one I experienced. Without proper treatment, Addison's disease will lead to death, but the prognosis for treatment is particularly good. The treatment consists of hydrocortisone, a pill that is taken every day.

The effect came a few days after I was released from hospital. Now, I had more energy than ever before. I had to jog several km a day to get rid of all the excess energy! It took a few days before my body became accustomed to this new reality, and the energy returned to more normal levels.

Was it really a miracle that I survived? Yes, I think so. Although many details have a natural explanation, God's grace played an important role here. My friends at church prayed a lot for me.

One particular memory that I will carry with me is from the hospital emergency room. After they had taken the blood samples and analysed them, one of the doctors came and stood in the doorway. He was looking at me in silence for a long time. Eventually, he spoke.

"You're not feeling well, are you?" he said with a serious face. By the way he looked at me, he thought I might die any moment.

One might ask the question of: why does God allows suffering from serious diseases, such as diabetes, particularly as a Christian? I believe things happen in this world, just as it rains on both rich and poor. I don't think Christians are immune to misery and hardship. Nevertheless, God's grace is with us, both in hard times and in good times!

Today, 27 years later, I have none of the complications that often follow diabetics. My diabetes doctor is quite amazed every time I see him. I can do my job without restrictions and travel as usual (when there are no travel restrictions caused by a pandemic, of course).

Today, there are advanced tools that greatly simplify life with diabetes. One example is the sensor on my arm, measuring my blood sugar level continuously without the need for blood samples. Another is the insulin pump, which automatically distributes the correct amount of insulin, around the clock. I am still awaiting my miracle for a healing, but meanwhile, these gadgets come in handy.

May 1994. The photo was taken a few
days before I sought medical attention.

11. The adventure in Kenya

That feeling of being at the wrong place...

Come with me to the spring of 1995, when I heard about a request for a sound technician in a large local church in Mombasa, Kenya. At that time, I was one of the sound technicians in a Stockholm church and was curious about this exciting challenge. A few phone calls later, it was decided that I would go there for a trial period of a few months. In August of the same year, it was time to embark on the journey. The church in Mombasa covered my travel expenses as I could not afford it myself.

Just over two weeks before my journey, I decided to pray for safe travel, all the way to Mombasa. Now, I will try to describe a few things that might be somewhat difficult to explain to someone who is not used to living close to Jesus.

Imagine we are praying for the journey, while picturing the different stages of the itinerary. At the image of almost arriving, I got a truly clear feeling, like a kind of threat. Whatever it was, there was an uneasy feeling throughout.

After praying about it for about half an hour, I had an equally clear feeling of the threat disappearing. Something might happen, but now I knew it would end well.

When I landed at Jomo Kenyatta airport in Nairobi, a local pastor picked me up and took me to the bus terminal to catch the bus to Mombasa. One of my fears was my luggage being stolen. The crew agreed to lock my bags in a special compartment, where only the driver had the key. The bus trip went well, even though it took all day to drive the 302 miles (486 km) on the bad roads. Towards the evening, after dusk, we finally approached Mombasa.

Wait a minute, where was my stop? Nobody had told me where to go, and Mombasa is a big city! The easiest thing was to get off the bus when everyone else did, that must be the bus station, right?

When we got to a place where all the other passengers got off, I followed. That was a big mistake. After I got off and got my bags, the bus drove away. That feeling of being left alone in a foreign country, in another continent, and in the wrong place…

It turned out that I had got off the bus a little too early and was now at Mwembe Tayari, in downtown Mombasa. It is a hub for the local buses and a place that was notorious for robbery and assault…

It is a very unsafe place to after sunset, especially for a white person who isn't familiar with the area. It was now almost 8 PM and dark. Everyone who came there with the same bus as me, got on their local buses and left. Then I was alone.

Now, I realized what I had been praying for, two weeks earlier. That definite feeling of things ending well remained, but what should I do? I could feel the atmosphere growing hostile and saw several people watching me from a distance with an increasing interest. I knew it was only a matter of time before that feeling would turn into a real threat.

Several people approached me and offered me a ride. I rejected them all, not being comfortable with the idea of following someone who insisted they knew who I was, despite me being in the wrong place. After a few minutes, I saw a taxi that looked safe. I stepped in and discovered that the taxi driver was a part of the church I was going to, Jesus Celebration Centre (JCC), in the Buxton area.

The church consisted of a large tent (like a circus) and seated over 4000 people. The area was guarded by a security guard, armed with bow and arrow. When I asked him for Pia Lindh, the Swedish missionary who would pick me up at the bus station, he told me she would be back soon. She and a colleague of hers had gone to pick up a visitor at the bus terminal (me, that is). A quarter of an hour later, Pia came back, and was very relieved to see me.

Her exact words were, *"You're alive! And you haven't been robbed!"* Pia told me they had been waiting at the bus station when the bus from Nairobi arrived. The bus driver told them that the only white man who had travelled on the bus from Nairobi had got off at Mwembe Tayari. They got in the car and hurried there as fast as they could. When they got there, they met someone they knew; he had seen me step into a taxi.

Despite living in Mombasa for several years already back then, Pia never left the car at Mwembe Tayari as it wasn't safe. She knew of several people who had been both robbed and severely beaten there. I am so happy that God's protection was covering me this time too!

During the four months I was in Mombasa, I began understanding why wonders and miracles occur much more often in these countries than back home. They have a completely different hunger for God and a heart that is not indoctrinated by the godlessness we see everywhere here in the Western world. It creates the conditions to be touched by God in a way that we rarely see in Europe.

When an African has been touched by God, he or she tells it to relatives, neighbours, friends, and everyone who wants to listen. Once, when the pastor of the JCC was shopping in a grocery store, he saw a leader of a Hindu temple. The man from the temple smiled at him and said happily, *"Congratulations, I hear your God is doing miracles in your church."*

It is true, our God is doing miracles, even today!

Outside Arlanda Airport in Stockholm, August 1995.
My journey to Mombasa has begun.

12. Front row seat

Like when the wind blows on a wheat field...

I want to tell you about one of the most powerful encounters with God I have ever experienced. It happened in Mombasa, Kenya, back in the autumn of 1995. For four months, I was working there as a sound technician in a large local church with over 20 000 members. Nowadays, they have a real church building, but back then it was like a large circus tent, seating over 4000 people.

Every Sunday was a meeting marathon like no other place I have visited. The church arranged services from 6AM to 6PM, every week. Each service lasted one hour and 45 minutes. By African standards, it is a real achievement to be able to hold a meeting within the allotted time. When one meeting was over, the 4000 people inside the tent changed places with another 4000 people, waiting outside. Despite the number of people, the exchange of people only took 10 minutes.

The PA system and mixing desk was my workplace; it was built on a high bench in the middle of the tent. From there, I had the front row seat and saw everything that happened in the church.

Imagine this big tent church, packed to the brim with people. They sat on simple benches, without backrests. The convenience we take for granted in the western world was not found there, as ushers placed as many people as possible on every bench. The benches were placed so tight that you had your knees in the back of the person it in front of you, while you had a couple of knees in your back yourself. The ushers did a good job, maximising the number of people in a limited area.

Some 15 minutes after the previous meeting ended, the worship team went on stage again, leading the next group of people in praise and worship. Kenyan people love music, and it is played loud. At the front of the stage were two tall stacks of speakers. The volume on the first row of seats was painfully loud. I don't understand how the people sitting there endured the high volume; it was louder than you would expect at a rock concert. The amplifiers were placed in an air-conditioned room, else they would have overheated.

When the praise and worship started, everyone in the church joined in, in a way I will never forget. All the people sang along, dancing, jumping, and bouncing like popcorn, to the beat of the music. Everyone, even the toddlers, jumped for joy. The worship team was often led by a Swedish missionary named Pia Lindh, and she led with an energy you don't see too often.

Jesus Celebration Centre often had guest preachers visiting on regular basis. The one I will talk about now came from Nigeria. I don't remember his name, but I will never forget one of his meetings. It was at the evening meeting, on the third day of the conference, when he said, *"Now, let us invite God to visit us with his Holy Spirit, in a special way."* He had announced this earlier, so expectations at the meeting were high. After preaching a short sermon, the praise and worship continued in the crowded tent. Everyone in the meeting stood up and praised God when HE showed up.

What I saw is best described as when the wind blows on a field and the wheat waves in the wind. But this is not about crop, it's about people. Suddenly, God's presence came upon a group of some 50 people, who collapsed under the power of God.

I have seen people falling under the power of God before, but never in such large crowds. One second later, another and larger group, collapsed, some 200 people.

And then it happened again and again, and within a minute several hundred (if not a thousand) people had come under the power of God so powerfully that they could not stand on their feet.

I consider myself a rational person, and of course I have tried to analyse this afterwards. What happened here, right in front of my eyes? Was it mass hypnosis? Or mass hysteria? What tricks did the preacher use? What did the pastor and the worship team do? Had everyone gone crazy?

I can only speak about what I saw and experienced. The presence of God is not easy to explain, but sometimes it feels like the air is filled with an oil mist and vibrates. Another way of experiencing it is like a weak electric current running through your body, without either cable or electricity. The guest preacher and the pastor both kept a low profile when the Spirit of God was visiting, and they welcomed Him without being an obstacle.

The worship team on stage continued to lead the praise and worship. Not the easiest thing to do, as some of them were under God's power so powerfully that they could hardly stand up.

The ushers were quite busy, removing benches so the people did not lie on top of them. Several of the ushers also fell under the power of God, but those who could, began to remove the benches and put them outside the tent. There were people everywhere, it almost looked like a bomb had gone off! But there was no blood here, only people who were overwhelmed by God's presence. And no one got hurt as they fell.

There are several reasons why I don't believe in mass hysteria or anything similar. The first one is, you do not want to fall on the stamped earth floor that was in the tent. When people came back to their senses and got up again, they were dirty from all the dust, but deeply affected. The second reason I believe it was God who visited His people is the result of the meeting with God they had experienced.

Several people testified about how they had got rid of pain and diseases, without anyone praying for them. Other witnesses said severe anxiety they suffered from had left and never returned. In the days after, I even heard people saying how they had been allowed to visit Heaven for a while. If it is possible to make such things happen with mass hypnosis or mass hysteria, I think we need more of it, especially when sick people recover!

In the Bible it is written in several places, how God visited his people in a special way. One of them describes what happened when the Temple was inaugurated in Jerusalem. The first book of Kings tells us in chapter 8 that, "...the priests could not perform their service because of the cloud, for the glory of the Lord filled his temple."

Back to the tent in Mombasa, where most people came to their senses again after a few minutes of their encounter with Jesus. Several people were so deeply affected that they were like in a Godly trance for up to one hour. The meeting continued with uninterrupted praise and worship for a while. No one was in a hurry to leave as everyone enjoyed the presence of God. As for me, I was also deeply touched, even though I did not collapse like many others. My experience is that you can have a powerful meeting with God on the inside, without it being visible on the outside.

The next day I had the opportunity to talk to Pastor Wilfred Lai and the guest preacher, asking what happened the previous night. Both said that when the Holy Spirit comes to visit it is so powerful, it is time to take one step back and let Him perform the works and miracles as He wishes.

The only thing we can do is have a surrendered and expectant heart. There was no special 'trick' to start what happened. God knows our hearts and responds to the cries of our hearts.

There was nothing unpleasant that night in the tent in Mombasa. The air was filled with a lovely atmosphere that cannot be easily described. Everyone present was filled with His presence and felt so incredibly good, like you only do in the presence of our Almighty God. I have experienced many powerful meetings of God myself, both at home and in church meetings.

Don't forget that God is a true gentleman. He is happy to visit, but only if He feels welcomed. And you don't have to worry, God can touch you without you falling on the ground!

13. Finding a wife

The lady with the most beautiful eyes I've ever seen

After turning 20, I was ready to get married. At least, I thought so myself. The problem was finding someone to spend the rest of my life with. This is probably familiar to most people; everyone hopes to meet the 'Right One', as soon as possible. Not many people want to waste time, energy and emotions on a relationship that doesn't last.

Some of my friends have found their spouse quite quickly, but unfortunately, they are in the minority. My own experiences weren't fun neither. The list of relationships includes both ordinary, nice girls and a pathological liar. But enough talking about that.

When I started my walk with Jesus in 1985, my future wife was a frequent subject of prayer for me. When could I meet her? Why does it have to take so long? Why should it be so complicated? The questions were many. Eventually, I concluded that I could wait until the time was right, but I needed a sign so I could relax.

After spending some time in prayer, I had a vision. It was not as spectacular as it may sound, it was an image that came to my heart. Imagine that you take a portrait of a beautiful woman and crop the photo so only her eyes are visible. No facial features, no hair, just a pair of beautiful eyes. That's exactly what I saw. Immediately, I understood that the beautiful eyes I saw belonged to my future wife.

The first time I saw Britta was at a tent meeting in Haninge, in the autumn of 1987. This happened just a few weeks after I moved to Haninge, so there were many unknown faces. I noticed her beautiful eyes immediately and asked a friend if he knew who she was. *"Her name is Britta,"* he replied. And she was not married…

Looking back at this many years later, one wonders why it would take so long before I connected Britta's beautiful eyes with the vision I had a few years earlier. And of course, there was a couple of reasons why it took several years before we got together.

In the autumn of 1998, I started giving computer lessons in evening classes, while looking for a permanent job. I saved a large portion of my salary to be able to negotiate better with my lenders. On 6th December, Britta and I got together. When I proposed to her (9th February 1999), I could use those savings and start planning our wedding. We did not have to borrow a penny.

Britta and I got married in on 15th May 1999. We had the Bible word Proverbs 18:22 in our hearts all day: *"He who finds a wife finds what is good and receives favour from the Lord."*

It was a beautiful, cloudless spring day and the whole world smiled on us when we stepped out from the church after the wedding ceremony. Afterwards, the guests told us even the birds rejoiced. Suddenly, they started chirping and singing to the full, the minute we came out on the church landing. It's a special memory.

Another special memory is from the reception, when the hostess dropped our three-storey wedding cake on the floor.

What an anti-climax!

Better yet, it was a practical joke, but my mother did not buy it at all! She said: *"That is not a real cake! They are too heavy to carry like that."*

She was right, but the applause when the real cake was brought in through the door, suggested that most people did buy the joke. One of the guests exclaimed happily *"How fortunate, they had another cake!"*

Looking back over the 22 years we have been married, it has not always been beautiful weather and smiles in our marriage. We have had our difficulties in agreeing on different things, and sometimes it has been a struggle.

Somehow, we have managed to find a way forward together, even in the darkest moments. Mutual respect has been one of the keys to not giving up when it was tough. And with increased respect, love grows.

14. Blizzard and ice

It happened on highway 70, north of the city Hedemora

What I am about to tell you happened in December 2002, as we visited Britta's family outside the Swedish city of Rättvik, the weekend before Christmas. We had bought our car a few months earlier, it came equipped with stud-less winter tyres. You see, in Sweden, legislation requires you to have proper winter tyres during the winter season, should the weather conditions require it. Driving from Stockholm was a nice cruise, with beautiful weather and 217 miles (350 km) of sunshine and nice, dry roads.

Britta turned restless every time we came near a lorry loaded with timber. I did find it a bit strange as she had never cared about lorries before. She tried to explain what she sensed, but I found it difficult understanding what she meant.

During the weekend I felt a growing anxiety that had no natural explanation, like a premonition of something terrible, waiting to happen. I decided to pray this through.

Now I will use an expression that may be new to you, namely *"prayer burden"*. It is a strong and supernatural urge from God to pray. As a Christian, you can get it when God wants to do something and needs our help. Yes, sometimes God needs our help; you can read more about it in the chapter *"Briefly about prayer"*.

This prayer burden was so heavy that I did not know if I would be able to bear it. It took several hours of prayer before I finally had a breakthrough. Now I knew that something might happen, but I also knew that it would end well.

Saturday saw rain and on Sunday afternoon the temperature dropped, with wind and snow. The wind increased in strength to a full blizzard.

The weather report on the TV news said this blizzard was now severe, advising against any road travel, unless absolutely necessary. We were obliged to go home, there was no alternative as the next day was a workday for both Britta and me. The blizzard was strong, with the snow falling more horizontally than vertically. The only things visible from the road were two black tracks in the snow. Knowing that it could be ice as well as asphalt didn't make things any better.

Some half hour drive from the city Hedemora, it happened. We were on road 70 and the speed limit was 90 km per hour (56 mph). I was driving at 80 (50) when the wind suddenly pushed the car, almost off the road. The car was now sliding sideways, dangerously close to the ditch.

Fortunately, I am an experienced driver even on icy roads, and knew instinctively how to handle the situation. The slide was parried, but there would be more of them. The road was now passing open fields where the wind gained speed and continued to push the car sideways. The storm forced the car sideways, and we slid and skidded several times, before finally reaching Hedemora.

We were, of course, startled over what happened. We stopped at a petrol station to have a cup of coffee and calm ourselves down a bit. The blizzard was forecast to stay for a few more hours, but we decided to continue our journey home, despite the bad weather.

Just after we passed the roundabout next to central Hedemora, it happened again. The car was gaining speed when a strong gust of wind suddenly pushed it from the left, now harder than ever before. The car was sliding violently, even though I was driving slowly at 70 (43). If I failed to manage to straighten the car, I would lose control of it. We would then spin and slide over to the wrong side of the road, where a lorry, fully loaded with timber, was approaching.

Not many people would survive such a crash. I fail to describe the feeling during that critical moment. Everything was in slow motion before the car finally straightened up on the road again. It only took seconds, but it sure felt like minutes. Britta was so scared that she wept, and I was so full of adrenaline that I was absolutely wide awake! We still had 150 km (93 miles) left to drive back home.

The rest of the trip went well. The blizzard settled into a calm snowfall. When we finally returned home a few hours later, we felt like we had won our lives back. It is impossible to describe the happiness we felt. We had survived the blizzard!

Thank you, Jesus!

15. Falling off a balcony

...he was clinging to the balcony railings from the outside

This happened during a weekend in the autumn of 2005. Once again, I come to things that can't be explained easily, please excuse me for this. For a whole day I carried a disturbing feeling, a premonition that something bad was about to happen. The feeling could not be ignored, so I began to pray, having no idea what I was praying for. This is often the case with prophetic intercession, you understand afterwards, when the person you have prayed for, tells you what he or she went through.

As the evening came, the prayer burden became heavier and heavier, with the feeling of seriousness becoming more and more apparent. In the end, I was in intense prayer, but it felt like I could not manage to pray this through. Suddenly, the prayer burden ceased, and was replaced by God's peace, an indescribable sweetness. I looked at the clock, it was just after 10PM.

The next day I called my good friend Conny, who lives in Eskilstuna. It was a few weeks since we spoke on the phone. Before I had a chance to speak about what I experienced the day before, he told me about a strange thing that happened to him. The night before, he had been drinking heavily. After the 10PM news, he stepped out onto his balcony to get some fresh air and was so tired that he leaned against the balcony railing.

And there he fell asleep, leaning over the balcony railing. You can probably guess where this story is going; he fell off the balcony and was desperately clinging onto the balcony railings, from the outside.

Conny lives on the fourth floor. As he began to realize the seriousness of the situation, he lost his grip and fell headlong, straight down.

Luckily, the landlord had removed the bushes right under his balcony just a few days before. The ground was muddy and soft after the day's rain, so he landed quite gently. *(I can imagine the splash he made when landing in the mud!)* Next to the place where he landed is a paved walkway that he barely missed.

My obvious question was how had he managed to fall without hurting himself? The only injury he got was a scratch on his forearm, as he hit the wall during the fall from the fourth floor!

Now the problem was that he did not have his key with him, and the front door was locked. He had to walk some 20 minutes away, without shoes, to someone who had a spare key he could use.

I was thrilled to tell him about the prayer burden I had struggled with at the very same time as he fell. I know that the angels of God helped in protecting my friend, falling without breaking every bone in his body. There is no way his survival could just be down to luck and chance.

What fascinates me is the feeling of being able to be of benefit in the Kingdom of God, in a way that affects other people in a positive way. Despite all my faults and shortcomings, God, in His grace, has chosen to use me. And not just me. He has a plan for every human being on our planet. We are infinitely precious in His eyes; Jesus' highest desire is to become your friend.

16. Water-powered drilling

A job offer with perfect timing

After working at Grindex for over ten years, I received an offer to work for the parent company, helping one of the business units with their communication. For a long time, I felt it was time for something new, so I was happy to accept this offer. Both the higher level of responsibility and the higher salary.

The 3rd of May 2010 was my first day at work. Already during the first week, it felt like I had ended up in the wrong place. Let's skip the details, but there were several things that didn't turn out like I had anticipated.

During the following year, I became increasingly unhappy at work. Eventually, I concluded that I had to find another job. Both me and my prayers became more and more desperate. How could I find my next employment?

One turning point came on a sunny day in August 2011, while driving to our cottage. It took some 90 minutes of driving to get there, and while Britta fell asleep in the passenger seat, I started praying quietly. Earlier, I had reasoned with myself and concluded that it was a good job, after all. Maybe I should try to get along with it?

As I prayed over it while driving, I clearly sensed a *'no'* on the inside. It really was time to leave, despite being a difficult decision to make. In my opinion, you should have a new job lined up before you resign from your current one. Risking becoming unemployed was not an enticing thought, so this situation was quite uncomfortable to me.

Monday morning came and I informed my boss of my decision to leave the company. If we could make some kind of deal, he could find a person to replace me faster. A few days later, he made me an offer which I accepted. My last day at work would be a few weeks later, Friday, 7th October 2011.

Earlier that year, after the summer holidays, I heard that a former boss of mine was resigning, leaving within a month. When talking about it, I told him about my decision to leave this company also, quite soon. *"If you need my skills, I will soon be available,"* I said.

Finally, my last day at work came, and it was time for me to hand over my computer, keys, and such. This Friday ended with the traditional farewell and various courtesies. As I was clearing the table after the coffee and getting ready to go home, my phone rang.

It was my former boss. *"I have discussed our situation with my boss now, and he approved my request to employ a Communications Manager. I have a job offer for you,"* he said.

My heart rejoiced and I responded with a *'Yes'* immediately. I had no idea about that company, apart from I knew it was a subsidiary of the largest mining company in Sweden, with an office in downtown Stockholm. We agreed that my first day at work would be on Monday, 7th November, so I got a month off before I started my new job.

On the first day at this new job, I already knew I was in the right place. During the introduction, I understood that this company had invented a new way of drilling with water-powered equipment. The handling of compressed air was both expensive and inefficient in mining operations, so this new drilling technology was saving a lot of money, while providing a much better work environment.

The technology was proven to work well in other applications as well, such as ground stabilising during foundation work. Now, the company needed help to deliver the message to the construction industry.

The decision was made to develop a completely new corporate identity, with a brand-new logotype and all. A brand agency developed a completely new style for us, while another agency helped develop new sales literature and a good website. After completing this work, our marketing material no longer looked like it represented a small garage company.

The next step was to get editorial coverage in trade media. My knowledge and connections from previous years with the same tasks came in handy. It was not long before the international construction and mining magazines knew about us and wanted to know more. I wrote several technical articles, explaining the water-powered drilling process in layman's terms, enabling the understanding of uninformed readers. It was exciting to receive information from the R&D department and explain it to the market.

The Bauma exhibition in Germany, April 2013, was the peak. Bauma is the world's largest construction and mining fair, taking place in Munich every three years and has over 2000 exhibitors from all over the world. I did most of the work myself, booked the floor space and designed the booth.

Three months prior to the fair, a large press meeting was organised, where exhibitors could meet editors from the trade media. Numerous editors accepted the press material I had prepared for them. We achieved good editorial coverage from multiple trade magazines, and I enjoyed myself highly.

Once again, I realise how easy and obvious everything sounds when describing it. And once again, I must say that this did not happen by itself. For a while, the prayer burdens were coming one after another, and my frustration of not seeing any change was obvious.

But he who prays, receives. God has repeatedly shown His grace and mercy with me as I chose to follow Him. This is just one in a series of all the interventions I have witnessed over the years.

At this point, I wonder if you agree with me; one simply can't say I've just been lucky all these years!

August 2013, a park in downtown Stockholm.
Steel rods are installed while drilled all the way down
to the bedrock, stabilising the ground. This picture was
published in several trade magazines.

17. A reluctant new business owner

"I've been recommended to call you. Can we meet?"

At the end of the summer of 2015, I began feeling that something in my professional life was about to change. It was a premonition, but I could not put my finger on it. The story of how I got this job at a subsidiary of Sweden's largest mining company is another miracle. I enjoyed that work so much, but now, a good four years down the road, it was time to move on.

In October, a friend of mine came with a clear message from Heaven, a prophecy: *"God has something new for you!"* he said. One typical characteristic of a prophecy from God is that it confirms what you already have in your heart. And that was true.

But it didn't turn out quite the way I imagined. During the autumn, my employer had to make financial savings as directed from the parent company; they had to lay off employees. They wanted to hire new staff, to be able to expand as planned, but instead they were forced to downsize and make people redundant. Four people had to leave their jobs and three had already left. One more person needed to leave, and that was me.

I left the company a few days before Christmas and got plenty of time to review my options. I had 15 years of experience in marketing, but no training. Without a formal degree in marketing communications, it would be difficult, almost impossible, to find a new job in that profession. My long and broad experience would not weigh heavily when compared to education.

What if I started my own business instead? Many years ago, I was employed at a company where I was, practically, self-employed. It ended with a financial crash that took 20 years to recover from, so I was very reluctant to the idea. First, I did not want to be self-employed. Secondly, I did not have a good business idea. So, no thank you!

However, this idea could not be brushed off, instead it kept coming back to me again and again. The more I prayed over it, the more I felt peace growing in me. Maybe starting my own business was not a bad of idea after all... I started thinking about how to make it a reality. Was it even possible?

I will never forget that day, at the end of February 2016. After Britta left for work, I sat down for a moment of prayer and began to speak what was on my heart:

"Dear Jesus, You know my heart inside and out. Holy Spirit, You know that I do not want to start a business. I do not want to, but I understand that You want me to do it. So now, I lay down my resistance to that idea."

*"**I choose to trust You**, despite my mind saying something else. **I choose to obey You and start my own company**. But, if this is not your plan for me, please show me so clearly, before it's too late. Because I can't handle another financial crash."*

I fail to describe the PEACE I felt in my heart after praying. Heaven had spoken! Now I could start working on implementing this idea. I decided not to take out a loan, so everything must be done simply and very cost-effectively.

I knew I could get some expert assistance from the insurance company that my previous employer is affiliated to. Among other things, they helped me to complete my application for a 'start-your-own-business' grant, which was crucial for me. This grant is a governmental aid, helping start-ups, covering part of your salary for the first six months.

It was not easy at all to get approval of the grant. It took me three visits to the job centre before even finding an employment agent who saw the possibility for me to manage my own business. Meanwhile, I had prepared a business plan and developed a budget.

As I describe the process of starting my business, I understand if you get the impression that everything just took care of itself; I took it easy and had a cup of coffee while God fixed everything for me…

But that was certainly not the case. Several times, I carried a prayer burden so heavy I didn't know how to bear it. Some things required prayers for not only days but weeks before I had a breakthrough to victory.

It is a particular feeling to be praying for hours in a row, without experiencing any change. It takes perseverance, time after time. Yet, it's also important to mention the feeling when you finally see a breakthrough. When you become so filled with God's sweet presence that you 'just know' it's done.

I prayed for several hours, day after day. When I finally had a breakthrough, I usually had no idea of what I had been praying for. I just 'knew' it was complete, and knew I was making progress, as strange as it may sound. And, sure enough, every time, something happened that brought me closer to my goal.

In the end, it was finally completed. My application for the 'start-your-own-business' grant got approved. At the end of May 2016, I registered my private business. I soon got some customers from previous connections, but I realized these wouldn't be enough, especially once the grant period would end.

I made some calls to my business network contacts, informing them about my company and my offer. I also called some of my connections abroad, mostly out of courtesy.

One of them, an American gentleman working in London, was always very polite and friendly. *"If I hear of anyone needing your services, I'll recommend you to them"*, he said. I remember smiling at his kindness. I didn't think he could do much to help me. But I was wrong; his gesture became a key factor in the success of my business.

One week after I registered my company, I received a phone call from an English gentleman. He called from an international trade association, looking for a representative in the Nordic region. I didn't understand why he had called me, but agreed to meet him the following week, when he would be attending a conference in Stockholm. At our meeting, he informed me the organisation's objective was to promote the safe and effective use of mobile elevating work platforms (MEWP's) around the world. This trade organisation was looking for ways to expand into Nordic and Baltic countries and needed help with doing this.

They offered a long-term contract of 10 days a month, to be renewed every year. I promised to consider this and get back to him a few days later. When I got home, I did some research about the organisation. I discovered it was established in 1983 and 90% of the world's MEWP manufacturers were members. With over 1200 members globally back then, they already enjoyed a large trust. And they needed my help to reach out to the Nordics...

My task is to recruit members and to promote their operator training. A challenge that suits me perfectly! The contract involves a lot of travelling, both within and outside the Nordic region.

Connecting with numerous rental companies and such, I plan and do all the travelling myself. The first years were quickly filled with travel, by air, rail, and road.

When the pandemic hit, my travels ceased. In the beginning of March 2020, after spending a week travelling in Finland, I was told there would be no more travel for a while. Instead, I have been able to work on other projects, such as translating the training material into Swedish. My contract was reduced for a few months, but I have managed to fill that void with supporting other customers.

It is no exaggeration to say that I have done well, despite the difficulties. Today (May 2021), I'm looking forward to travelling again, even if it will take time before everything goes back to normal.

Looking back over the past five years, I cannot cease to be amazed. Back then, I had, of course, no idea about the things I have been describing here. Not even in my wildest imagination could I compete with what is now a reality. What if I had refused to start my own business, or declined to meet the Englishman? If so, none of this would have happened...

God's sovereign plan is getting clearly visible here, of course He knew all about this, and well in advance. He planned it more wonderfully than I could wish for. I 'only' had to do my part to make it happen. Today, looking back on the prayer burdens I finally managed to pray through, I'm so glad I didn't give up.

I cannot convey all the details of this story as it would fill a book. I remember many of them, especially the feeling that God was building something good for me while I was praying. It really wasn't just a 'castle in the air'!

One memory is of producing the logotype for my company. It is often a long and expensive process, so I wanted to postpone it a bit. Then, a company that I used to hire many years ago (when I was employed), offered to produce a logotype for me. They even produced business cards and a small brochure for my sales visits. And they did everything for free, in just one month!

Another special memory was my visit to Switzerland to sign my contract. There I sat, a new entrepreneur, ready to sign a contract that exceeded my dreams. For a second, I remembered lying on my bed 24 years earlier, completely destitute and without any hope. That period is forever gone from my life and now was the time for me to take the next step.

I became so emotional that I had to bite my lip, keeping the tears from falling. Luckily, I managed to keep a cool face and rejoiced over what was waiting. And now, I enjoy continuing that journey.

A clear example of an **unsafe** handling of a MEWP. The gate in the basket has been tied up so nothing is preventing the user from falling out of the lift. In addition, he has stepped out of the basket at height, despite it being illegal.

18. My first prayer trip: to Pakistan

*I know better than anyone else, I can
not cure even a fly on my own!*

In February 2017, I spent ten days in Lahore, Pakistan. Those days gave me warm memories for life. I want to tell you something about this journey, and what made me travel to this country. The Swedish Ministry of Foreign Affairs advised against *"unnecessary visits"* to Pakistan, due to disturbances and threats from violent Muslim groups.

For starters, I have no personal interest in going to any Muslim country, for obvious reasons. In addition, it is far away, with flights over eleven hours to get there. No travel guide on Pakistan could be found in the bookstore. When I googled travel stories from the country, I only found adventurous people, wanting to go to somewhere completely different than the usual tourist destinations.

When I was invited to go there, my spontaneous thought was *"No, no, never!"* Then, something happened on the inside of me, a feeling that can partly be explained as curiosity, but mostly with that soft voice of God in one's heart. Reluctantly, I agreed to pray over the matter. If God approved of the idea of travelling to Pakistan, I would go, otherwise I would not.

I have already stated that I would be dead and buried a long time ago, had it not been for God's intervention, several times. Since I wouldn't be alive today without the grace of God, it's not hard to give Him my life. *"I no longer live, but Christ lives in me"* (as Paul writes in Galatians 2:20).

The idea of travelling was quite easy to resist, at least I thought so. But instead, a longing grew in my heart to go. Finally, after praying for a few days, I decided to stop resisting and follow my heart, and travel to Pakistan.

My first intention was not to tell anyone about this journey as I paid for everything myself and didn't need any financial aid. However, during my preparations I realised I could raise money for food packages for poor families in the villages we would visit. Reluctantly, I contacted friends, who responded with a big heart. The money I collected was enough for 108 different food packages with basic items, in different sizes. After returning home, I was happy to post photos on Facebook of all the happy recipients of the food packages.

Although I looked forward to helping poor families, I carried something else in my heart. Imagine praying for the sick and seeing them recover. Imagine being able to see someone who has been affected by various obsessions become free from them. I know it sounds crazy to someone who isn't used to believing in wonders and miracles, but I know who I believe in! And I remember so well all the miracles I have experienced first-hand.

I also saw the journey as an opportunity to see if God can work miracles through an ordinary person, like me. What if only one person gets better after intercession? If so, I think it's worth it. Then at least I have done the little I can do to help. I want to emphasise that I have never guaranteed anyone a miracle; I have no right to do so. But I believe that Jesus works wonders even today!

During my stay in Pakistan, we arranged a meeting every day, seven days in a row, in the early afternoon. Everywhere, we saw a hunger for God among the people. We never told anyone about the handing out of food packages in advance.

At one point, more than 50 people huddled together in a small apartment for our meeting. People were sitting everywhere, leaving hardly any room to stand as I got up to preach. The electricity went off for a while, continuing the meeting in the light of battery powered lights until the power came back. No one complained. Everyone wanted to stay and listen when I spoke about how God can use ordinary people. Like me, that is.

In every meeting, I also invited for intercession. *"If you have a problem in your body or soul, I would like to pray for you, if I may,"* I said. Each time, people lined up to be prayed for. I was able to pray for a total of 150 people during my trip. All kinds of problems were prayed over, from muscle pain, joint pain, and vision problems to problems with compulsory thoughts and nasty family members who caused problems at home. Everyone received intercession with warm gratitude.

You see, I have come to a point in my life where I am confident that Jesus works miracles today. Otherwise, I would be crazy to pray for people like this. I know better than anyone else, I cannot cure even a fly on my own! But I do not walk alone. I pray in Jesus' name, and see things happen.

Later, I received reports of more than 15 miracles. Most apply to pain that has subsided, sometimes after causing trouble for years. Other testimonies relate to high blood pressure decreasing to normal, and in some cases, a financial situation that was suddenly resolved in a supernatural way. I know some people are too shy to speak about themselves receiving help from Heaven, while others consider the problem is solved 'on its own'. I saw myself how God touched people mightily when we prayed for them.

Earlier in this book, I described how I experienced the power of God in 1985, when the Holy Spirit came over me with His power. On this journey I experienced the grace to stand in that power myself, conveying wonders and miracles to people in a completely different country, several days in a row. I KNOW that Jesus works today, HE deserves all the glory! I'm just a channel for Him, He is the one who knows and makes everything happen!

There are so many more things I could tell, much more than I can fit in here. In all this, one thing is obvious to me:

Nothing beats the feeling of walking with Jesus on His adventures!

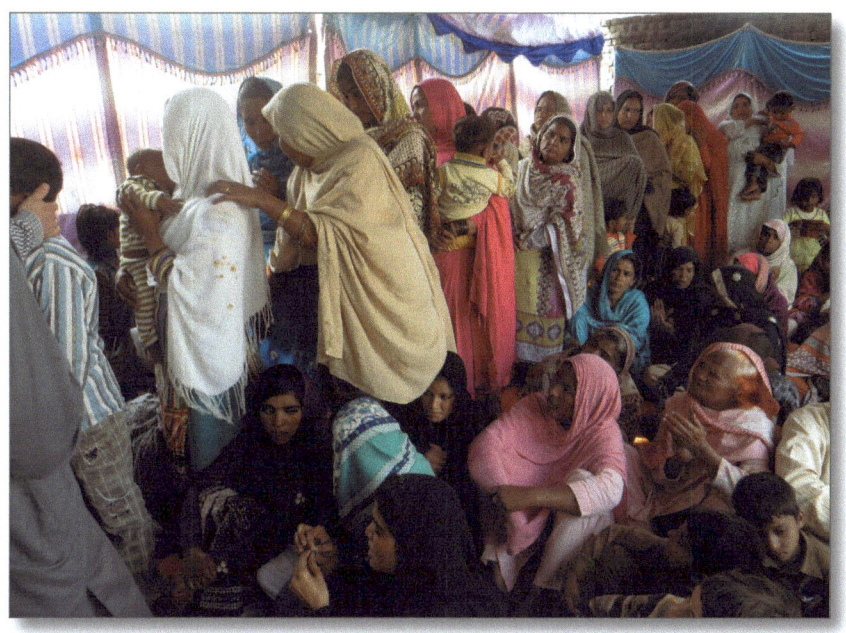

People queueing for intercession in Rangpura Sialkot, Pakistan. In the far left, you can see my hand as I'm praying for a boy.

19. And finally…

I am not the cool one!

In this book I am sharing some of my most personal experiences. I have chosen to step out of my comfort zone and be very upfront. These stories cover only some of my personal experiences; there are so many more I could talk about. And there are, naturally, quite a few of mistakes, negative events, and their details as well, but I choose to focus on these good ones.

Many personal testimonies give the impression that life becomes perfect and wonderful once someone becomes a Christian and allows Jesus to lead him or her through their life. That has not always been the case for me. Problems have occurred, and some have been difficult, although I have caused most of them myself. However, Jesus has also been present, helping me through everything. HE is a big reason that I am still alive.

Many of these stories have never been told before, as they are close to my heart. I only relay my own experiences, without adding anything. What I have experienced doesn't need any extra spice.

You see, I am not the cool one! The one who deserves all glory is Jesus Christ, He who died for all of us on the cross, 2000 years ago. I do understand if you are amazed over what God has done, and continues to do, in my life. Believe me, I am also amazed at His grace. It really is Grace alone.

Every human being is unique, right? Despite that, please understand one thing: I'm no more special than anyone else. Despite my name, I am not a superhero; superpowers are not present in my life. In myself, I have nothing to brag about. The wonders and miracles in my life did not happen thanks to me – *rather, they have happened despite me.*

The one thing I have done is making an active choice; to always be open hearted for God to lead me through life. It is important to me to be close to Jesus, to want to spend time with Him. He who already knows everything about me but still loves me.

A personal invitation

It's more than 40 years since I made an active decision to become a Christian. After my discovery of the New Life, everything else became somewhat uninteresting. That's typical of me; hesitating and considering for a long time before making any big decision. But once I have decided, it is all or nothing.

I would like to invite you to get to know Jesus. If you say yes to Him, it will be a journey that will change your life. When Jesus is invited, He comes with a sweetness that fundamentally changes people. In Revelation 3:20, Jesus says: *"Here I am! I stand at the door and knock. If anyone hears my voice and opens the door, I will come in and eat with that person, and they with me."*

The image of a meal is used as it is such a pleasant event, where everyone involved enjoys themselves. Jesus is like that; everyone feels so Heavenly good when you are in His presence.

Over the years, I have met many people who don't come from a Christian family (and, of course, many who have chosen the Christian faith from a young age, as well).

Those who have made the greatest impression on me are people who have come from misery and now live a life of restoration. Several of them are former criminals, the kind of people that society prefers to see behind bars. In their life story, one sees how Jesus has changed them completely in a way that can neither be denied nor used to avoid the consequences from their past lives.

These people met Jesus when their lives were at their worst. People who had to fight their way through prison sentences and other hardships. The change in them is obvious, even several years after they surrendered to Jesus.

But God also wants to meet *YOU*. When Jesus died on the cross, it was for all the people on Earth. You, and me, and everyone else, without exception.

John 3:16-17 says: *"For God so loved the world that he gave his one and only Son, that whoever believes in him shall not perish but have eternal life. For God did not send his Son into the world to condemn the world, but to save the world through him."*

When I discovered it really is true, it was not long before my decision to start living for Jesus. If He was willing to die for me on the cross 2000 years ago, I am willing to live for Him today, and for the rest of my life.

The Bible says that we, as human beings, are created in the image of God and that we need to return to the fellowship with Him for which we were created. Since God makes no difference between us, I know He wants to transform your life as well. If he may do so, of course.

We must dare to accept His forgiveness. The Bible states, in the Book of Acts 10:38 that *"Jesus went around doing good and healing all"*. We must dare to believe that He wants us well.

You are saved by making a conscious decision, accepting Jesus as Lord in your life. Be completely honest and turn to Jesus Christ. You can pray in your own words or repeating this short prayer. Read this, aloud to yourself:

Jesus, I come to you now.

Thank You for forgiving all my sins.

I receive You as Lord and Saviour.

Jesus, I give you my whole life and I thank You for giving Your life for me.

Lead me into the life You intended for me.

Amen

If you prayed this prayer from your heart, you are now saved, another word for a Christian.

Congratulations!

The Heaven rejoices over you, just as it says in Luke 15: 7.

This is a moment that can be emotional for one person while another person may not notice any particular feelings. The most important thing is to believe, and trust, in Jesus Christ. The Bible makes a promise to you in John 1:12: *"Yet to all who did receive him, to those who believed in his name, he gave the right to become children of God."*

To move forward in your Christian faith, I recommend you contact a local church, one that believes that Jesus performs miracles today.

I also recommend attending an Alpha course. Alpha is an 11-week course that creates a space, online or in person, where people are excited to bring their friends for a conversation about faith, life, and God. It is an environment where questions are encouraged, and you can ask anything.

They also arrange meetings online, have a look at www.alpha.org

God Bless You!

A. A briefly word about prayer

Can we have a communication with God? And does He answer? Here, I want to share my image of prayer and mention a few things I have discovered.

At first glance, prayer may be the most meaningless thing one can do. Speaking straight into the air, to someone you do not see. And then, addressing your circumstances, giving them orders…

For someone without a relationship with Jesus, this is often how prayer is perceived – a touch of folly. The factor of prayer is often brushed off. Someone once said: *"Nice that you have been able to speak about your worries. Not that there is a god that hears you, but still…"*

In the Western world, people often roll their eyes when I mention the power of prayer. But for those who believe in Jesus, prayer is one of the most powerful ways of life, available on this planet. It becomes even more obvious when our prayers are answered and an impossible situation changes.

To begin with, there are different kinds of prayer. Some of them are praise, worship, fellowship with God, thanksgiving, and praying for a change. Here I am focusing on the prayer that wants to change something.

Let's divide this kind of prayer into two subparts; the one that I initiate myself, and the prophetic one. The prayer I initiate myself is based on my own will to see a change, from my perspective. It may be the need for a new job, healing from illness, guidance from God, or something else. This is the kind of prayer most people associate with the word *"prayer"*.

The prophetic prayer is on a different level, as God takes the initiative for it. When God has planned something good for us, we need to do our part of the work. It might be regarding a need you don't see yet, or in the event of impending danger. The one thing they have in common is you often have no idea what to expect, but you still need to pray. The Holy Spirit is the one who knows everything, and we need to choose to trust Him.

How will He be able to lead me, without me knowing what the concern is? Romans 8:26-27 says: *"In the same way, the Spirit helps us in our weakness. We do not know what we ought to pray for, but the Spirit himself intercedes for us through wordless groans. And he who searches our hearts knows the mind of the Spirit, because the Spirit intercedes for God's people in accordance with the will of God."*

There are different ways it can be done. What I have mentioned a few times is *"prayer burden"*.

What is a prayer burden?

The easiest way to explain a prayer burden is a Heavenly call to pray for a change. God puts a concern in our heart, even though it is not a common concern. Quite simply, it is a recurring call to pray. The human mind does not go far when we walk with God; it's too easy to manipulate. Therefore, God places the call to pray deeper than that, in our innermost being.

The way a prayer burden feels like may differ from person to person. It can be like a kind of anxiety that is not emotional and can't be explained psychologically. One of several characteristics is that I can say *'no'* to a prayer burden. It can also be silent for a period when I need to rest. When a prayer burden is completed, one is often filled with a Heavenly Peace from God, transcending all understanding.

Praying through

The most effective way to handle a prayer burden is to *'pray it through'*. This expression comes from the early Pentecostal revival, when the biblical principle was applied, and people prayed until they saw the result. In other words, **they prayed until it was done.**

Several stories in the Bible describe how Jesus prayed for many hours, and sometimes at night as well. If Jesus needed to pray so much to see God's will manifested in his life, then we as Christians need to pray too. Only then can we see God change things in our lives at the level He wants.

The 'legal' aspect of prayer

Why can't God fix all things himself? If He has no limitations, surely, He doesn't need our help, does He?

We need to remember that God gave this planet Earth to us human beings. It is our property, and we are the ones in charge. (This is simplified; the reality is more complex.)

Some people think that God can't change things, or He simply doesn't care. That is not true! God both wants and can, and He cares for us so much more than we will ever understand.

Imagine someone receives a house as a gift. When the donor pays a visit, he must respect whether a room has been rebuilt or painted in other colours than he intended. God respects us and our free will, even when it goes against what He had planned. He is a very friendly person.

Hence, when I pray for someone, I invite God to come and do what He wants most of all, namely helping people! Every Christian is God's ambassador!

God wants to bless us; the question is
whether we allow Him to bless us?

B. My view of the supernatural

All that glimmers is not God

Nowadays, God is nearly completely abolished in the Western world. The supernatural is mostly spoken of by people involved in occult contexts, like 'New Age'. The word *"supernatural"* itself is mostly associated with magic, divination, ghosts, and other strange things. As a result, many people lack an understanding of the healthy supernatural and find the subject generally unpleasant.

I have met several people who have witnessed supernatural things. It's often a simple thing, such as an intuition. You come to think of an old friend just before they call you on the phone. There are also stronger expressions. Once, I heard about an icy wind, passing through a room, in the middle of a warm summer's day with the windows closed. The people who experienced it was talking about a relative who had recently passed away, when strange things started to happen and the atmosphere in the room turned uncomfortable. It was an unhealthy supernatural event.

I understand if people find these types of experiences exciting; there are several TV shows about the 'supernatural'.

But have you ever heard anyone talk about how amazingly good they feel after a session, and how worries and nightmares stopped tormenting them? It does not happen, for the simple reason that it is not the power of God creating these types of experiences.

There are healthy supernatural events, and there are unhealthy ones. How do you know the difference? One easy way is to ask how people feel afterwards. Do they feel so Heavenly good as you do in the presence of God, or does it feel more uncomfortable?

The Bible tells us how it all began, in Genesis, chapter 3, God said, *"You must not eat fruit from the tree that is in the middle of the garden, and you must not touch it, or you will die."*

We know how that story ended. Adam and Eve ate the forbidden fruit and died. But did they really die? The Bible tells us that they lived on even after they fell into sin. How can this be?

Man consists of spirit, body, and soul. Our body is quite obvious to us. As for the soul, we know it's hosting our mind and our emotions. Reasoning, logic, and memories are some other functions of the soul. All these functions survived the fall of Adam and Eve, even if they were affected.

When mankind fell in sin, the spiritual connection to God died. After that, man could no longer have the kind of fellowship with God that we were created to have. This applies to all people. The Bible states in John 4:24 that *"God is spirit…"*.

Not only did Adam and Eve lose touch with God, but they also allowed evil to enter this world. Before the fall, there was no shortage, suffering, distress, or death. Everything was wonderful. This is no longer the case, and we see examples of it everywhere.

The Bible says that the human spirit needs to be born again. In John 3: 3, Jesus says, *"Very truly I tell you, no one can see the kingdom of God unless they are born again"*. Today we call it becoming a Christian and being saved.

I know several people who have been active in different occult activities. Every one of them states that life as a Christian is so much better than their old life, in every way. They experience an inner peace that was not there before. The occult world is both dark and evil, not to be played with. My absolute recommendation is to stay away from any occult activity, without exception!

You see, it's not possible to find any darkness in the presence of God. The Spirit of God can fill someone to such an extent that you almost want to ask Him to turn it down a bit. I know this from personal experience. In His presence you feel so Heavenly good that you just want to linger as long as possible. In the Gospel of Mark chapter 9, Jesus shows his glory to some of his disciples. Peter wanted to build booths on the site, so they could stay in God's presence even longer.

In this book, I've been sharing some of the supernatural things I've encountered. Another example of a healthy supernatural is when you pray for someone and receive a prophetic word from that person. I see the supernatural as 'God's natural'. It becomes natural in a way that cannot be explained.

When you become a Christian, you enter a healthy supernatural relationship with Jesus. How it looks differs from person to person, depending on your personality and calling.

We need to understand that one kind of it is not 'better' or more valuable than another. You do not become 'more' Christian because you experienced certain things. God loves us all 100%, just as we are.

But it's also easy to walk astray. When you start seeking guidance in the supernatural instead of seeking Jesus, you quickly get the wrong focus. There are Christians who want to interpret everything as supernatural. *"If the water tap drops three times, I have to go shopping,"* is one funny example. That's not what I am talking about.

Conclusion:

God is naturally supernatural, but He is never unnatural!

C. Discovering your calling

When the calling from God takes your heart captive

Imagine having a calling from God for your life, but you don't grasp it. How would you describe something that has been in your heart for decades? Is it even possible to explain? I want to tell you about my own journey of discovering my calling, hoping that someone can get a little an insight about their personal calling.

The Bible describes, in Acts, chapter 9, how Saul met Jesus so radically that his whole life took on a whole new direction. It also tells of a man named Ananias, who received a prophetic message from God. Who was this man?

It starts in verse 11: *"Go to the house of Judas on Straight Street and ask for a man from Tarsus named Saul, for he is praying. In a vision he has seen a man named Ananias come and place his hands on him to restore his sight."* A little later in the text, we follow Ananias when he prays for Saul, who later takes the name Paul.

Some important details are revealed here:

1. God can use whoever He wants. This man, Ananias, isn't mentioned anywhere else in the Bible and was probably not a member of a church leadership group. My guess is that he was an ordinary Christian, with a heart to serve God.

2. God can speak very specifically. Both the address and the name of the person who needed intercession were completely correct. Everything turned out just as God said.

3. God chooses to use ordinary people. When we obey God's guidance, we get to see His miracles and wonders.

Nowadays, I feel a bit like Ananias, enjoying praying for the people and situations the Lord wants me to pray for. A calling can be clear, like an evangelist who can't help but talk about Jesus. Some callings are lifelong while others may be for a shorter period of someone's life. We all have a place in God's amazing plan.

Examples of the more 'invisible' callings are people who volunteer to do the practical duties that often remain unseen. We usually never think of who cleans the church premises. I can think of one particular lady, who was responsible for the cleaning team in a church I attended for many years. You could tell she enjoyed what she was doing. Year after year, she stayed faithful to her task. She did it with all her heart and she never asked for praise. She knew she was doing it for Jesus. When the time comes, He will reward her for the work she has done for the Kingdom of God.

In my own life, the calling was not always obvious. I realised I had a calling in the beginning of autumn of 1985, six months after my first meeting with God. A longing began to take shape; I wanted to do something for Him who has given me His life. At first, it was unclear but then it became clearer – I mean, the knowledge that I had a calling became clearer. The calling itself was still unclear. It was frustrating not to see what I would do with this longing that had taken my heart captive.

I discovered you can't invent your own calling, because it is God who places it in you. The expression says it all: *"called by God"*. Yet, I tried to do just that, inventing my calling. Decided I was probably called to be a missionary. But where should I go? Maybe to Africa, like the classic image of a missionary? I will not go into details, but I did try a few things. If time travel were possible, I would tell myself (back in the 80's and 90's), to focus on being really close to Jesus instead. HE will tell when and what to do, and until then, we just need to spend time with Him.

I went to Kenya, working as a sound technician, in the autumn of 1995. I considered it a soft start before moving on to become a missionary. Nowadays, looking back, it feels more like God took me there to show me that my calling was not as a missionary. It takes a certain type of person to cope with everyday African life, and I didn't do that very well. Besides, I had a mess waiting for me here at home, with large debts after my financial crash.

During my time in Mombasa, I had plenty of time to consider my situation. I came to realise the need to take care of my own life instead of trying to escape reality. Back home in Sweden, the plan was clear: first get an education, then get a job and start paying off my debts. The call wouldn't go away for that.

Fast forwarding to spring of 2004, I took a course in gift discovery. The course was called *"Like the fish in the water,"* based on the book *"Network Participant's Guide: The Right People, in the Right Places, for the Right Reasons, at the Right Time"* (published by Willow Creek). In a systematic way, you go through what aptitudes you have naturally, and in what way you enjoy serving God.

The image of myself as a potential missionary soon faded. Instead, another image began to emerge, and it became much clearer. I always loved praying, enjoying seeing things change, both in my own life and in the lives of others. It was easy to see a pattern in my personal life.

At the end of the course, we were asked to select some good friends, not attending this course themselves. They were given a questionnaire from the book, where they could give their view of me as an individual. All of them concluded, independently, that my calling seemed to be in the realm of prayer. When summing up the course, it became clear to me; *I was called to intercession.* After 19 years, I had finally found my place in God's plan.

Let me be clear with one thing here: no one told me what conclusion to make about myself. It wasn't a 'lottery' or anything goofy. It was completely my own conclusion. The book and the course helped me to put things in context, where I could start evaluating factors in a way I could not have done on my own.

I began to tell other friends what I had realised, a bit tentatively. Everyone agreed with my conclusions. Finally, after trying it thoroughly in my heart, I began to become more and more open to my calling. I became more confident and had the opportunity to serve in different ways.

The calling of an intercessor has several advantages, one is it combines the work of a regular job very well. My favourite places to pray are during travelling. With worship music in my headphones, it's quite easy to shield yourself from the world for a while, regardless of whether you are sitting on a bus or in an airplane.

During the preparation for my journey to Pakistan, I saw the opportunity to pray for people, but also to teach about prayer. Since then, opportunities have opened up in several places. I have also been able to teach and pray for people in Germany, the United States and, most recently, in India. We will see what opportunities come in the future.

I am very keen to teach about prayer, seeing the principle of *"give the poor a fishing equipment instead of fish,"* working well here. Today, many people want someone else to pray for their problems. I was doing this myself, turning to well-known preachers, asking for their intercession. But the Bible is clear that God has no favouritism to a person. He hears prayer from children as well as prayer from other people.

When you are a professing Christian, the Bible says that you have the right to come before the Throne of God, asking for His help. Thus, every Christian can pray and receive answers to their prayers. When I realised this, the search for someone who could do the prayer work for me ended. Instead, I make sure to pray things through, myself.

Finally, a piece of advice to those of you who know you are carrying a call, but don't see the details: stay close to Jesus and listen to what He leads you to do! And look for patterns in the ways you enjoy serving God.

One clear pattern for me was I repeatedly acted as an intercessor in different situations. And attending a course, like I did, is another good way.

D. Thank you

First of all, I want to thank my dear wife, Britta, for putting up with me. Multiple times, I've prayed my way through these *prayer burdens*, causing her to ask what I am up to. She finds it a bit concerning when I can't tell her what or who I am praying for, however, when we see the result, we rejoice together.

Writing your memoirs involves several challenges. It is completely different to telling them in person. To begin with, the whole personal part with gestures and the way of speaking is lost. In addition, the text must not be full of grammatical errors. Starting a sentence with *and*, or *but*, works well orally but not necessarily in writing.

Then, comes the extra effort and obstacles when translating the text to English. Being a native Swede, writing a book in my second language holds a few challenges!

I am so grateful to my friends *Faith C* and *Brian K* for their help in corrrecting the worst grammatical errors.

From the bottom of my heart, THANK YOU!

Kent